CAT BREEDS

SPHYNXES

BY ABBY DOTY

WWW.APEXEDITIONS.COM

Copyright © 2025 by Apex Editions, Mendota Heights, MN 55120. All rights reserved. No part of this book may be reproduced or utilized in any form or by any means without written permission from the publisher.

Apex is distributed by North Star Editions:
sales@northstareditions.com | 888-417-0195

Produced for Apex by Red Line Editorial.

Photographs ©: Shutterstock Images, cover, 1, 4–5, 6–7, 8–9, 10–11, 12, 13, 14, 15, 16–17, 18, 19, 21, 22–23, 24, 25, 26–27, 29

Library of Congress Control Number: 2024944886

ISBN
979-8-89250-316-7 (hardcover)
979-8-89250-354-9 (paperback)
979-8-89250-429-4 (ebook pdf)
979-8-89250-392-1 (hosted ebook)

Printed in the United States of America
Mankato, MN
012025

NOTE TO PARENTS AND EDUCATORS
Apex books are designed to build literacy skills in striving readers. Exciting, high-interest content attracts and holds readers' attention. The text is carefully leveled to allow students to achieve success quickly. Additional features, such as bolded glossary words for difficult terms, help build comprehension.

CHAPTER 1
PARTY ANIMAL 4

CHAPTER 2
BREED HISTORY 10

CHAPTER 3
CUTE AND CURIOUS 16

CHAPTER 4
CAT CARE 22

COMPREHENSION QUESTIONS • 28
GLOSSARY • 30
TO LEARN MORE • 31
ABOUT THE AUTHOR • 31
INDEX • 32

CHAPTER 1

PARTY ANIMAL

A girl starts cleaning. She is getting ready for a birthday party. Her sphynx cat comes into the living room. The cat sits on the couch to watch.

Sphynxes often follow their owners from room to room.

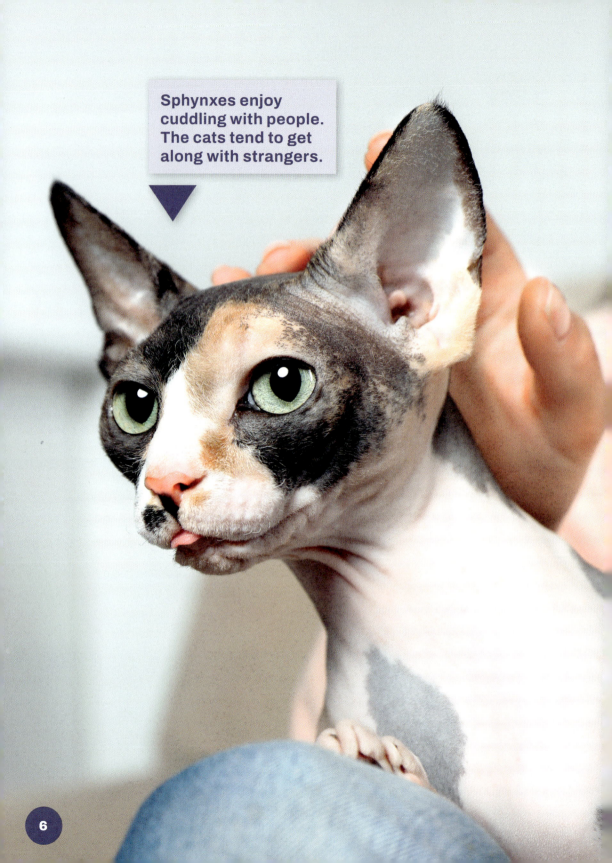

Sphynxes enjoy cuddling with people. The cats tend to get along with strangers.

Soon, the girl's friends arrive. The sphynx **purrs** and rubs against their legs. The guests take turns petting and holding him.

CAT ALLERGIES

Some people are **allergic** to cat **dander**. Dander often gets on cats' fur. But sphynxes shed very little. So, people with allergies may have an easier time being around them.

Most sphynxes are active and playful.

FAST FACT

Sphynxes are social cats. They get along with most children and pets.

8

Next, the kids take out a feather toy. The sphynx leaps toward it. He swats at the toy. The cat plays for hours.

CHAPTER 2

BREED HISTORY

In the 1960s and 1970s, several hairless kittens were born in the United States and Canada. They had a **mutation**. This **gene** caused a lack of hair.

Sphynxes were originally called Canadian hairless cats.

People liked how the kittens looked. So, they had the hairless cats **mate** with Devon rexes and Siamese cats. Those **breeds** had short fur. A new, hairless breed began.

Early sphynxes had health problems. Crossing sphynxes with other breeds made healthier kittens.

Donskoys are another hairless breed. They were created in Russia in the 1980s.

HAIRLESS BREEDS

Sphynxes were not the first hairless breed. Hundreds of years ago, **Aztecs** had hairless cats in Mexico. All those cats died out. But people bred several other types of hairless cats.

Sphynxes became an official breed in the early 2000s.

Sphynxes spread to different parts of the world. People loved the friendly and playful cats. The breed became very popular.

FAST FACT

Sphynxes were named after **mythical** creatures from Egypt called sphinxes.

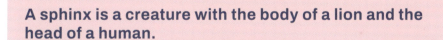

A sphinx is a creature with the body of a lion and the head of a human.

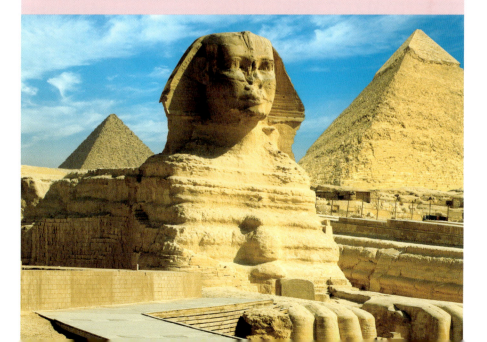

CHAPTER 3

CUTE AND CURIOUS

Sphynxes are medium-sized cats. Most sphynxes weigh less than 12 pounds (5 kg). The cats have large ears and large eyes. They also have long, thin tails.

Most sphynxes do not have whiskers.

Sphynxes look hairless. But they actually have very short, thin fur. Their skin and fur come in several colors.

A sphynx's short fur is very soft.

A sphynx may need to wear a sweater to stay warm in winter.

COLD CATS

Because sphynxes don't have much fur, they tend to get cold easily. Owners can put sweaters or blankets on their cats. Sphynxes may also lie in sunny spots to warm up.

Sphynxes are curious. They enjoy exploring. The cats often jump and climb. Owners may need to keep breakable things off shelves.

FAST FACT

Many sphynxes like to sit in spots that are high above the ground.

Some sphynxes sit on their owners' shoulders.

CHAPTER 4

CAT CARE

Despite their short fur, sphynxes actually need more grooming than many other cats. Their skin can get oily. So, many sphynxes need baths every week or two.

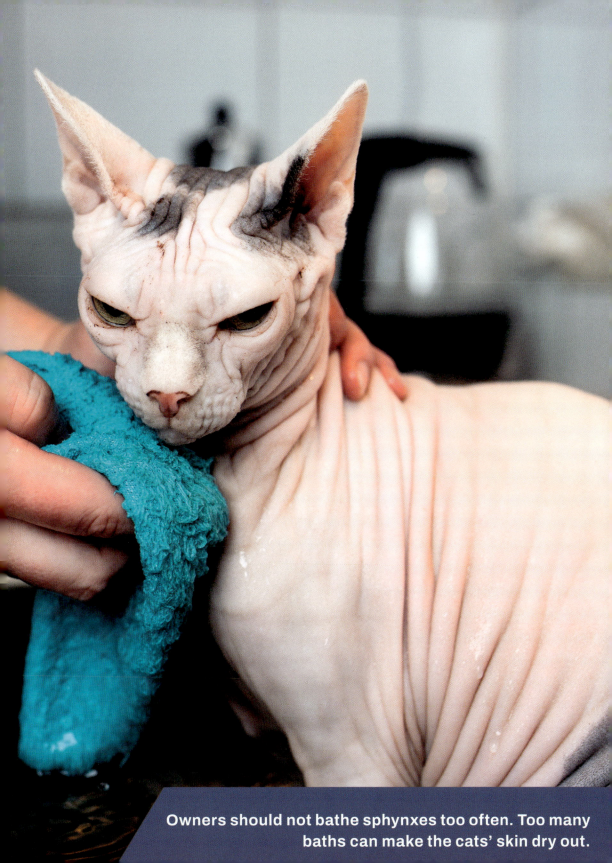

Owners should not bathe sphynxes too often. Too many baths can make the cats' skin dry out.

Some sphynxes learn to walk on leashes.

Sphynxes are indoor cats. They can get sunburned easily. So, owners should put sunscreen on the cats if they go outside.

FAST FACT
A sphynx's ears get dirty easily. Owners should clean them once a week.

Dirt or wax can get caught in a sphynx's ears or skin folds. Owners can remove it gently.

Sphynxes need lots of attention. Owners should play with their cats every day. And they shouldn't leave them alone very long.

NEEDY CATS

Sphynxes get lonely easily. So, many owners choose to get two sphynxes. That way, the cats can keep each other company when their owners leave. Toys and scratching posts can also help sphynxes stay busy.

COMPREHENSION QUESTIONS

Write your answers on a separate piece of paper.

1. Write a few sentences explaining the main ideas of Chapter 4.

2. Would a sphynx be a good pet for your family? Why or why not?

3. How often should owners clean their sphynxes' ears?
    - A. never
    - B. every day
    - C. every week

4. What kind of cat would be most difficult for people with allergies to be around?
    - A. a cat that does not shed much
    - B. a cat that sheds a lot
    - C. a cat that does not have dander

5. What does **exploring** mean in this book?

Sphynxes are curious. They enjoy exploring. The cats often jump and climb.

    A. resting and sleeping often
    B. moving and looking through an area
    C. staying in one place all day

6. What does **company** mean in this book?

So, many owners choose to get two sphynxes. That way, the cats can keep each other company when their owners leave.

    A. being unsafe
    B. being alone
    C. being with others

Answer key on page 32.

GLOSSARY

allergic
Reacting to something by feeling sick.

Aztecs
People from an empire that ruled large parts of Mexico from the 1300s to the 1500s.

breeds
Specific types of cats that have their own looks and abilities.

dander
Flakes of skin that get on an animal's fur or hair.

gene
A tiny part of a cell that controls how an animal looks.

mate
To form a pair and come together to have babies.

mutation
An unexpected change in a gene.

mythical
From stories or myths, not real life.

purrs
Makes a low, vibrating sound.

BOOKS

Clausen-Grace, Nicki. *Sphynx*. Mankato, MN: Black Rabbit Books, 2020.

Jaycox, Jaclyn. *Read All About Cats*. North Mankato, MN: Capstone Publishing, 2021.

Pearson, Marie. *Cat Behavior*. Minneapolis: Abdo Publishing, 2024.

ONLINE RESOURCES

Visit www.apexeditions.com to find links and resources related to this title.

ABOUT THE AUTHOR

Abby Doty is a writer, editor, and booklover from Minnesota.

INDEX

A
allergies, 7
Aztecs, 13

B
breeds, 12–14

C
Canada, 10

D
Devon rexes, 12

E
Egypt, 15

F
friendly, 14
fur, 7, 12, 18–19, 22

H
hairless, 10, 12–13, 18

M
Mexico, 13

O
owners, 19–20, 24–25, 27

P
play, 9, 14, 27

S
Siamese cats, 12
social, 8
sphinxes, 15

U
United States, 10

ANSWER KEY:
1. Answers will vary; 2. Answers will vary; 3. C; 4. B; 5. B; 6. C